Our Favorite
Food Gifts

Copyright 2017, Gooseberry Patch

Get new neighbors to come out of their shells by delivering
a batch of Maple Syrup Shortbread! Take over a list of
neighborhood grocery stores, dry cleaners, doctors,
dentists and hair salons. Add a map of the town and
circle popular shopping malls and movie theaters.

Maple Syrup Shortbread *Makes about 1-1/2 dozen*

1/2 c. plus 1 T. butter, softened
   and divided
1/4 c. sugar
1 c. all-purpose flour
3/4 c. brown sugar, packed

1/2 c. maple syrup
1 egg
1 t. vanilla extract
Optional: 1/2 c. chopped walnuts

Blend 1/2 cup butter and sugar together in a large bowl until light and fluffy. Add flour a little at a time, mixing continually; blend well. Pat mixture into a lightly greased 8"x8" baking pan. Bake at 350 degrees until light golden, about 25 minutes; remove from oven and set aside. Stir together brown sugar, syrup and remaining butter. Add egg and vanilla; mix until smooth. Pour evenly over baked shortbread; sprinkle with walnuts, if desired. Return to oven; bake at 350 degrees until topping sets, about 20 minutes. Let cool; cut into 1-1/2"x1-1/2" squares. Store in an airtight container.

Friendship Day is the first Sunday in August. Celebrate by
filling an old-fashioned milk carrier with 2 bottles of milk and
2 stacks of Mom's Italian Biscotti...tuck in some napkins
and surprise a friend with a yummy afternoon treat.

Mom's Italian Biscotti

Makes 3 dozen

5-1/2 c. all-purpose flour
1 T. plus 2 t. baking powder
3/4 c. butter, softened
1-1/2 c. sugar

6 eggs, beaten
zest and juice of 2 lemons
3-1/2 c. powdered sugar

Mix together flour, baking powder, butter and sugar; form a well in the center. Add eggs and zest; knead until dough is smooth. Shape dough into 2-inch balls on a floured surface; roll each into a 7-inch rope. Twist into knots; place on lightly greased baking sheets. Bake at 350 degrees for 15 to 18 minutes. Cool on a wire rack. Combine lemon juice and powdered sugar; drizzle over cookies.

Special Delivery! Copy vintage postcards and old letters
onto plain paper for easy personalized wrapping. Use a twisted
cord or jute as ribbon and tie on a shipping label for the gift tag.

Delectable Peanut Butter Squares

Makes one to 2 dozen

1/2 c. butter
1/2 c. brown sugar, packed
2 c. creamy or crunchy
    peanut butter

1 t. vanilla extract
2-1/2 c. powdered sugar
6-oz. pkg. semi-sweet
    chocolate chips

Melt butter in a large saucepan over low heat, stirring to prevent burning. Add brown sugar; stir until completely dissolved. Add peanut butter and vanilla; mix thoroughly. Add powdered sugar; stir well. Press mixture into a 13"x9" baking pan sprayed with non-stick vegetable spray; let cool. Melt chocolate chips in a double boiler over low heat; spread evenly over peanut butter layer. Let cool completely; cut into squares.

Crafty friends will love receiving a knitting gift basket. Pick out colorful yarn, needles in different sizes and an easy-to-make pattern. Pack all the materials in a handy tote that can be used for future projects. Don't forget to tuck in some Apple Butterscotch Squares to snack on while stitching!

Apple-Butterscotch Squares

Makes about 2 dozen

2 T. cornstarch
4 c. apples, peeled, cored and
    chopped
1 c. butterscotch chips
1 c. quick-cooking oats, uncooked

18-1/2 oz. pkg. yellow cake mix
3/4 c. butter, softened
1 t. cinnamon
1/2 c. brown sugar, packed
1/4 c. wheat germ

Combine cornstarch, apples and chips in a large saucepan; heat until chips
have melted. Set aside. Mix oats, cake mix and butter together until coarse
crumbs form; set one cup mixture aside and press remaining crumbs into
an ungreased 13"x9" baking pan. Spread apple mixture on top; sprinkle
with cinnamon. Combine reserved crumb mixture with brown sugar and
wheat germ; layer over apple mixture. Bake at 350 degrees for 35 to
45 minutes; cool at least 30 minutes. Cut into squares.

When making these treats for a bake sale, you can dress them up by using shaped cookie cutters to cut them, rolling edges in candy sprinkles or sprinkling lightly with colored sugar.

Caramel Crispy Bars

Makes 1-1/2 to 2 dozen

2 10-oz. pkgs. marshmallows
3/4 c. butter, divided
12 c. crispy rice cereal, divided

14-oz. pkg. caramels, unwrapped
14-oz. can sweetened condensed
   milk

Combine one package of marshmallows and half of butter in a large microwave-safe bowl. Microwave on high setting for 2 minutes. Stir until smooth; microwave for one more minute. Stir in 6 cups cereal; mix well. Press mixture firmly into the bottom of a greased 13"x9" baking pan using a greased spatula. In a microwave-safe bowl, combine caramels and condensed milk; microwave on high setting until caramels are melted. Stir until smooth; spoon over cereal layer. Use remaining ingredients to prepare a second batch. Press second batch of cereal mixture on top of caramel layer. Let stand for 5 minutes; cut into squares. Wrap each square individually with plastic wrap.

Personalize this giant cookie with the recipient's name
if you like, or decorate it with holiday designs!

Giant Chocolate Chip Cookie

Makes 8 servings

2 c. all-purpose flour
1 t. baking soda
1/2 t. salt
3/4 c. butter, softened
3/4 c. light brown sugar, packed
1/2 c. sugar

1 egg, beaten
2 t. vanilla extract
3/4 c. semi-sweet chocolate chips
3/4 c. milk chocolate chips
Optional: vanilla ice cream

In a bowl, whisk together flour, baking soda and salt; set aside. In a separate large bowl, stir butter and sugars until light and fluffy. Add egg and vanilla; mix well. Add flour mixture to butter mixture; beat just until blended. Stir in chocolate chips. Transfer dough to a lightly greased cast-iron skillet; gently flatten dough. Transfer skillet to oven. Bake, uncovered, at 350 degrees for 40 to 45 minutes, until golden on top and edges. Do not overbake. Cool cookie in skillet on a wire rack for 15 to 20 minutes; cut into 8 wedges. Serve warm; top each wedge with a scoop of ice cream, if desired.

Try baking Sweet Potato Fruit & Nut Loaf in 3-inch terra cotta pots for individual gifts. To prepare pots, coat insides with oil and bake at 350 degrees for 30 minutes; cool completely then repeat process again. Pour bread batter into foil-lined pots and bake as directed, reducing time by 10 to 15 minutes.

Sweet Potato Fruit & Nut Loaf

Makes one loaf

1-1/2 c. all-purpose flour
1-1/4 c. sugar
2 t. baking powder
1/4 t. salt
1 t. cinnamon
1 t. pumpkin pie spice
2 eggs, beaten
1 c. milk

1/2 c. oil
1-1/4 c. canned sweet potatoes,
  drained and mashed
1/2 c. maraschino cherries,
  drained and chopped
1/2 c. chopped pecans
1/4 c. golden raisins

Mix flour, sugar, baking powder, salt and spices in a medium bowl;
blend in eggs, milk and oil. Stir in remaining ingredients; pour into a
greased and floured 9"x5" loaf pan. Bake at 350 degrees for 45 minutes.
Makes one loaf.

Make a sweet toast to family & friends at the next breakfast
or brunch gathering. Just bake Cappuccino Muffins in paper-lined
mini muffin cups...stack 3 to 4 in a clear fluted glass and
set at each place setting. Charming!

Cappuccino Muffins

Makes one dozen

2 c. all-purpose flour
3/4 c. sugar
2-1/2 t. baking powder
1/2 t. salt
2 T. baking cocoa
1 c. milk

2 T. instant coffee granules
1 egg, beaten
1/2 c. butter, melted
1 t. vanilla extract
3/4 c. mini semi-sweet chocolate
     chips

Combine flour, sugar, baking powder, salt and cocoa in a large bowl;
set aside. Mix together milk, coffee and egg; stir into flour mixture. Stir
in butter and vanilla; mix well. Stir in chocolate chips. Spoon batter into
paper-lined or greased muffin cups, filling 2/3 full. Bake at 375 degrees
for 17 to 20 minutes, until a toothpick tests clean. Cool in pan for
5 minutes; transfer to a wire rack to finish cooling.

Use monogrammed linen napkins to wrap up several different loaves of bread...place the loaf in the middle, bring the corners up and tie with a bow, being sure the monogram can be seen. Place the wrapped loaves in a cheerful bread basket and deliver to newlyweds in their new home.

Rosemary & Onion Bread

Serves 6

1 loaf frozen bread dough,
    thawed
1 to 2 T. olive oil

1 to 2 t. dried rosemary
1/4 c. onion, chopped

Coat dough with oil; place on a greased baking sheet. Press rosemary and onion into dough. Bake at 350 degrees for 30 to 40 minutes, until golden.

Give this to the host of your next tailgate party! Turn any
favorite cheese ball recipe into a "football." Just shape, sprinkle
with paprika and pipe on cream cheese "laces"...so easy!

Parmesan Cheese Ball

2 8-oz. pkgs. cream cheese,
    softened
2/3 c. grated Parmesan cheese
2/3 c. walnuts, finely chopped
1/4 c. onion, finely chopped

1 T. milk
1/4 t. garlic powder
1/2 t. salt
1/4 t. pepper
1/2 c. pecans, coarsely chopped

In a large bowl, combine all ingredients except pecans. Stir together until well blended. Shape into a ball; roll in pecans to coat. Wrap cheese ball in plastic wrap; refrigerate for at least 8 hours or overnight. Let stand at room temperature about 30 minutes before serving.

Most muffin batters can be stirred up the night before, and can even be scooped into muffin cups. Simply cover and refrigerate...in the morning, pop them in the oven. Your new neighbors will love a basket of warm muffins welcoming them to the neighborhood.

Raspberry-White Chocolate Muffins

Makes one dozen

2 c. biscuit baking mix
1/2 c. white chocolate chips
1/3 c. sugar
2/3 c. milk

1 T. oil
1 egg, beaten
1 c. raspberries

Grease bottoms only of 12 muffin cups. In a bowl, stir together all ingredients, except raspberries, just until moistened. Gently fold in raspberries. Divide batter evenly among cups. Bake at 400 degrees for 15 to 18 minutes, or until tops are golden. Cool slightly; remove from tin to a wire rack.

Handy party favors! Nestle several Red Velvet Cake Balls
inside colorful party hats. Arrange the hats in a glass bowl
and let guests pick one up on their way out.

Red Velvet Cake Balls

Makes about 4 dozen

18-1/2 oz. pkg. red velvet
    cake mix
16-oz. container cream
    cheese frosting

16-oz. pkg. regular or white
    melting chocolate

Prepare and bake cake mix following package directions for a
13"x9" cake; let cool. Crumble cooled cake into a large bowl. Stir in
cream cheese frosting. Roll mixture into balls the size of quarters.
Place on baking sheets and chill for several hours or overnight. Melt
chocolate in a double boiler. Dip cake balls into chocolate and place
on wax paper. Let sit until firm.

Freeze to please! Make treats ahead of time and keep them frozen for last-minute gifts. Freeze pies up to 4 months, breads up to 3 months, cheesecakes up to 30 days and baked, unfrosted cookies up to 6 months. Be sure they are airtight, labeled and dated.

Autumn Spice Streusel Cake

Serves 8 to 10

18-1/4 oz. pkg. spice cake mix
1 sleeve graham crackers, crushed
3/4 c. brown sugar, packed

1/2 c. butter, melted
2 t. cinnamon
Garnish: powdered sugar

Prepare cake mix according to package directions; set aside batter.
In a separate small bowl, mix graham cracker crumbs, brown sugar,
butter and cinnamon; set aside. Lightly coat a 12-cup Bundt® pan with
non-stick vegetable spray. Pour half of batter into pan. Add all of crumb
mixture; pour remaining batter on top. Bake at 350 degrees for 35 to
40 minutes, until cake tests done with a toothpick. Let cool. Turn out
cake onto a cake plate; dust with powdered sugar.

Add a personal touch to a gift in minutes with letter beads.
Wrap a wide ribbon around a wrapped box of No-Bake
Maple-Peanut Drops, securing ends in back with tape.
Thread letter beads onto narrow ribbon to spell out a name,
and layer over the wide ribbon, knotting in back.

No-Bake Maple-Peanut Drops

Makes about 2-1/2 dozen

1-1/2 c. sugar
1/2 c. milk
1/4 c. maple-flavored syrup

1/2 c. creamy peanut butter
2 t. vanilla extract
2 c. quick-cooking oats, uncooked

Combine sugar, milk and syrup in a medium saucepan; bring to a rolling boil over medium heat, stirring frequently. Boil for 3 minutes; stir in peanut butter and vanilla. Add oats, mixing well. Drop by rounded teaspoonfuls onto wax paper. Cool for 3 to 4 hours until firm.

Wrap Creamy Butter Mints in wax paper and give
in a jadeite glass bowl...sure to bring back
memories of Mom's kitchen.

Creamy Butter Mints

1-lb. pkg. powdered sugar
1/2 c. butter, softened
2 T. whipping cream

1/4 t. peppermint extract
2 drops red food coloring

Place powdered sugar and butter in a medium bowl. With an electric mixer on medium speed, beat together for 2 to 3 minutes, until creamy. Add cream, extract and food coloring; beat for 3 to 4 minutes until well blended. Shape mixture into 1/2-inch balls; lightly press balls with thumb to form wafers. Place on wire racks and allow to dry overnight, uncovered. Store in an airtight container.

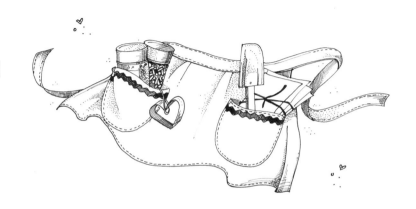

Make a gift basket for a beginning baker. Personalize a mini
apron with fabric paint and fill the pockets with cookie cutters,
a mini spatula, recipe cards and sprinkles...add it to a basket
with a batch of homemade Apple Pie Fudge for inspiration!

Apple Pie Fudge

Makes 2 dozen

3 c. white chocolate chips
12 gingersnaps, finely crushed
1/2 c. apple pie filling
3 c. sugar
3/4 c. butter

1 c. whipping cream
1/8 t. salt
1 t. cinnamon
1/2 t. nutmeg
1/2 t. allspice

Line a 8"x8" baking pan with parchment paper, leaving "handles" at each side; set aside. Combine chocolate chips, cookie crumbs and pie filling in a bowl. Beat with an electric mixer on low speed; set aside. In a large saucepan over medium heat, combine remaining ingredients. Bring to a rolling boil; cook, stirring constantly, for 4 minutes. Remove from heat. Quickly pour over chocolate chip mixture. Beat on medium speed until chocolate melts, about 2 minutes. Pour into pan. Refrigerate for 3 hours, until set. Lift fudge by paper handles to a cutting board. Cut into small squares.

This savory bread will be a welcome hostess gift any time of
year. Wrap it on a pretty cutting board as part of the gift!

Mexican Braid

1 lb. ground turkey
10-oz. can diced tomatoes with
     green chiles, drained
1 onion, chopped
1 c. corn

2 loaves frozen bread dough,
     thawed
8-oz. pkg. shredded Pepper
     Jack cheese

Brown turkey with tomatoes and onion in a skillet over medium heat; drain. Add corn; cook until heated through. Roll out each loaf of dough to 1/4-inch thickness. Transfer to baking sheets that have been lined with lightly greased aluminum foil. Cut diagonal slits along each side of the dough, about one inch apart and 3 inches deep. Place half of turkey mixture in the center of each piece of dough. Top each with half of cheese. Fold in short sides of dough, pinching to seal. Fold dough flaps over the turkey mixture, alternating sides and creating a braided pattern. Pinch edges to seal. Bake at 350 degrees for 25 to 30 minutes, until golden.

Pick the best from this year's garden...lettuce, cucumbers,
tomatoes, onions and radishes. Put them all inside a pretty
glass trifle bowl (it's beautiful for serving colorful salads)
and add a package of Homemade Soup & Salad Croutons.

Homemade Soup & Salad Croutons *Makes 4 servings*

1 T. butter
5 T. olive oil
2 cloves garlic, minced
1 t. onion salt

1 t. dried thyme
1 t. dried oregano
5 slices day-old bread, crusts
   trimmed

Melt butter with oil in a 12" skillet; mix in garlic, salt, thyme and oregano. Cube bread; sauté in skillet until golden. Drain croutons on paper towels; cool. Store in an airtight container.

A wonderful shower or housewarming gift. Wrap a doily
around a loaf of bread, tie with a fluffy sheer bow and deliver
with a crock of homemade spread to the tea party hostess.

Maple-Raisin-Walnut Spread

Makes 1-1/4 cups

8-oz. pkg. cream cheese, softened
1 T. chopped walnuts
1 T. raisins
1 t. water

3-1/2 T. dark brown sugar, packed
1/8 t. maple extract
1/8 t. cinnamon

Whip cream cheese until smooth; set aside. Grind walnuts coarsely in a food processor or blender; set aside. Place raisins and water in food processor; chop into small pieces. Combine raisin mixture and one teaspoon walnuts with cream cheese; mix well. Add remaining walnuts, sugar, extract and cinnamon; mix well, cover and chill until firm.

Turn a chip & dip bowl into a bread & spread server!
Just put a container of Homemade Boursin Cheese in the
middle (where the dip usually goes) and surround it with
toasted slices of baguette bread. Cover it all with plastic
wrap and take it along to your next neighborhood gathering.

Homemade Boursin Cheese

Makes 3 cups

2 8-oz. pkgs. cream cheese,
    softened
8-oz. container whipped butter,
    room temperature
1 t. garlic salt
1/2 t. dried oregano

1/4 t. dried marjoram
1/4 t. dried thyme
1/4 t. dried basil
1/4 t. dill weed
1/4 t. pepper

Combine all ingredients in a food processor or blender. Process until completely blended and smooth. Line a serving bowl with plastic wrap; spoon cheese mixture into bowl. Cover and refrigerate for several hours before serving, to allow flavors to blend.

This savory reminder of summer's bounty can be packaged
with a wedge of Havarti and a sleeve of crackers.

Sun-Dried Tomato Spread

Makes one cup

1 T. garlic, minced
1 T. olive oil
1/4 c. water-packed sun-dried
    tomatoes, drained and
    chopped

1/4 c. water
8-oz. package cream cheese,
    room temperature
snack crackers

In a small skillet on medium-low heat, sauté garlic in oil until softened. Add tomatoes and stir to coat; add water and simmer until tomatoes are plumped. Drain if necessary. In a bowl, mash tomato mixture into cream cheese. Serve on crackers.

Tuck a jar of Farmhouse Salsa and a bag of tortilla chips inside a big sombrero. Add a small piñata filled with candy... snacks and entertainment in one gift!

Farmhouse Salsa

3 15-1/2 oz. cans stewed
    tomatoes, chopped
8-oz. can tomato sauce
4-oz. can diced green chiles
2-1/4 oz. can black olives,
    chopped

1 bunch green onions, chopped
2 cloves garlic, chopped
2 T. rice wine vinegar
2 T. olive oil
4-oz. can jalapeño peppers,
    chopped

Combine all ingredients in a serving bowl; mix well. Cover with plastic wrap; refrigerate overnight.

Package a jar of Homemade Apple Pie Filling
with an ice cream scoop to remind your recipient
what goes best with warm apple pie.

Homemade Apple Pie Filling

Makes 4 jars

10 c. water
4-1/2 c. sugar
1 c. cornstarch
3 T. lemon juice
2 t. cinnamon
1/4 t. nutmeg

1 t. salt
2 to 3 drops yellow food coloring
5-1/2 lbs. apples, peeled, cored
   and sliced
6 1-quart canning jars and lids,
   sterilized

Combine all ingredients except apples in a large saucepan. Cook over low heat until thickened, stirring occasionally; set aside. Divide apple slices equally among hot sterilized jars; ladle thickened sauce over top, leaving 1/2-inch headspace. Wipe rims; secure with lids and rings. Process in a boiling-water bath for 20 minutes; set jars on a towel to cool. Check for seals; attach instructions.

Instructions:

Pour one jar filling into an unbaked 9-inch pie crust. Arrange a second unbaked pie crust over top; crimp crust and cut several vents. Bake at 350 degrees for 30 to 40 minutes. Serves 8.

Bring a gift for the brunch host. Pour Green Tomato-Pineapple Jam inside a simple lidded glass bowl...tie on an oversized ribbon to keep the lid secure and tuck a serving spoon into the knot.

Green Tomato-Pineapple Jam

Makes about 6 jars

4 lbs. green tomatoes, cored,
  peeled and thinly sliced
5 c. sugar
8-oz. can crushed pineapple
juice of 1 lemon

7 whole cloves
1 4-inch cinnamon stick
zest of 1 orange
6 1/2-pint canning jars and lids,
  sterilized

Combine tomatoes and sugar in a heavy kettle over medium heat; bring to a boil. Boil until tomatoes are soft, about 20 minutes, stirring often. Stir in pineapple; boil for 15 minutes. Add lemon juice and spices (in a spice bag); boil until jam coats the back of spoon, about 20 to 30 minutes. Discard spice bag. Spoon into hot sterilized jars, leaving 1/4-inch headspace. Wipe rims; secure with lids and rings. Process in a boiling-water bath for 15 minutes; set jars on a towel to cool. Check for seals.

A whole-grain loaf of bread or sweet angel food cake
adds a sweet touch to your homemade gift.

Grandma Klamm's Peach Butter *Makes about 12 jars*

10 c. peaches, peeled, pitted
   and quartered
5 c. sugar
1-1/2 t. cinnamon

1/2 t. nutmeg
12 1-pint canning jars and
   lids, sterilized

Working in batches, purée peaches in a blender; transfer to a slow cooker. Stir in sugar and spices. Cover and cook on low setting for 6 to 8 hours, raising lid so it is partially ajar about one hour before done. Peach butter is ready when it reaches desired consistency and turns a rich medium brown. Spoon into hot sterilized jars, leaving 1/4-inch headspace. Wipe rims; secure with lids and rings. Process in a boiling-water bath for 10 minutes; set jars on a towel to cool. Check for seals.

Sharing Mom's and Grandma's tried & true canning recipes is a great way to hand down favorite recipes that generations have loved. Keep the recipes, but be sure to update the preserving methods if needed. Some ways Grandma canned, using a wax seal or the inversion method for jams & jellies, are no longer a good way to keep foods their freshest.

Blueberry-Lemon Jam

Makes 7 jars

4-1/2 c. blueberries
6-1/2 c. sugar
juice and zest of 2 lemons

2 3-oz. pkgs. liquid pectin
7 1/2-pint canning jars and
  lids, sterilized

Combine blueberries, sugar, lemon juice and zest in a large saucepan over high heat; bring to a boil. Stir in pectin; bring to a rolling boil and stir constantly for one minute. Remove from heat; skim foam if needed. Spoon into hot sterilized jars, leaving 1/4-inch headspace. Wipe rims and secure lids and rings. Process in a boiling-water bath for 15 minutes. Set jars on a towel to cool. Check for seals.

When giving sweet preserves, don't forget to add a
loaf of homemade bread or muffins and creamy butter
so they can be enjoyed right away!

Mom's Blackberry Jam

Makes 4 jars

4 c. blackberries, hulled
4 c. sugar

4 1/2-pint canning jars and
lids, sterilized

Place blackberries in a large Dutch oven over medium-high heat; just cover with water. Bring to a rolling boil; add sugar. Boil until mixture drips thickly from a wooden spoon, about 30 to 45 minutes. Spoon into hot sterilized jars, leaving 1/4-inch headspace. Wipe rims; secure with lids and rings. Process in a boiling-water bath for 10 minutes; set jars on a towel to cool. Check for seals.

Whip up a picnic gift basket in minutes! Fill a retro picnic tin
with savory jams...perfect as sandwich spreads or
dips for veggies and bread sticks.

Firecracker Hot Pepper Jelly

Makes 6 to 8 jars

1 red pepper, cut into wedges
2/3 c. habanero peppers, chopped
1-1/2 c. white vinegar
6 c. sugar, divided

2 3-oz. pkgs. liquid pectin
6 to 8 1/2-pint canning jars and
   lids, sterilized

Place peppers and vinegar in a blender; cover and purée. Add 2 cups sugar; blend well. Pour into a large saucepan. Stir in remaining sugar; bring to a boil. Lightly strain mixture, discarding pulp, and return to pan. Stir in pectin. Return to a rolling boil over high heat. Boil for 2 minutes, stirring constantly with a wooden spoon. Remove from heat; skim off foam. Pour into hot sterilized jars, leaving 1/2-inch headspace. Wipe rims; secure with lids and rings. Process for 5 minutes in a boiling-water bath. Set jars on a towel to cool; check for seals.

Search flea markets for inexpensive glass relish trays
to pair with your pickles for one-of-a-kind gifts.

Teri's Carrot Cake Jam

1-1/2 c. carrots, peeled and grated
1-1/2 c. pears, peeled, cored and
    chopped
14-oz. can crushed pineapple
3 T. lemon juice
1-1/2 t. cinnamon

1 t. nutmeg
1 t. ground cloves
3-oz. pouch liquid pectin
6-1/2 c. sugar
6 1/2-pint canning jars and
    lids, sterilized

Mix all ingredients except sugar and pectin in a large saucepan. Bring to a boil over medium heat. Reduce heat to medium-low; simmer for 20 minutes, stirring occasionally. Add pectin and return to a boil. Stir in sugar; bring to a full rolling boil, stirring constantly. Remove from heat. Pour into hot sterilized jars, leaving 1/2-inch headspace. Wipe rims; secure with lids and rings. Process in a boiling-water bath for 10 minutes. Set jars on towels to cool; check for seals.

Here's an easy way to wrap up a jar of Cappuccino Mix!
Punch two holes in the folded-over flap of small paper luminaria
bags. Thread ribbon and decorations through the holes.

Cappuccino Mix in a Jar

Makes 4 cups

1 c. powdered non-dairy creamer
1 c. chocolate drink mix
3/4 c. instant coffee granules

1/2 c. sugar
1/2 t. cinnamon
1/4 t. nutmeg

Combine all ingredients in a mixing bowl; place in an airtight container.
Attach instructions.

Instructions:

Place 2 tablespoons mix in a mug; add 3/4 cup boiling water. Stir until
dissolved. Makes one serving.

Make a big butterscotch candy! Roll Butterscotch Bars in a Jar
in several sheets of yellow cellophane, twist each end and tie
with yellow ribbons. Glue a small piece of butterscotch candy
on a gift tag and attach to the jar...so clever!

Butterscotch Bars in a Jar

Makes 2 dozen

2 c. all-purpose flour
1-1/2 t. baking powder
1/4 t. salt
1/2 c. flaked coconut

1/2 c. sugar
2 c. brown sugar, packed
1/8 t. nutmeg

Combine flour, baking powder and salt together; set aside. Layer remaining ingredients in order listed in a one-quart, wide-mouth jar, pressing each layer firmly before adding the next. Add flour mixture to the top; secure lid. Attach instructions.

Instructions:

Place mix in a large mixing bowl; toss gently to mix. Add 3/4 cup softened butter, 2 beaten eggs and 2 teaspoons vanilla extract; mix until blended. Spread batter into a greased 13"x9" baking pan; bake at 375 degrees for 25 minutes. Cool. Cut into bars to serve.

Create a clever package for Wildwood Pancake Mix!
Fold a bright kitchen towel in half and sew 2 sides closed
to form a bag...slip the mix inside and tie closed with
jute. Don't forget to give with a big spatula for flipping!

Wildwood Pancake Mix

Makes about 10 cups mix

4 c. all-purpose flour
4 c. cracked wheat flour
1 c. sugar

2 T. baking powder
2 t. salt
1 c. lard

Combine all dry ingredients except lard; mix well. Cut in lard with a pastry cutter until well blended. Place in an airtight container; attach instructions.

Instructions:

Place 2 cups mix in a medium bowl. Add one beaten egg and 1-1/2 cups water to desired consistency; stir until moistened. Heat a buttered skillet over medium-high heat. Pour 1/4 cup batter into skillet for each pancake. Cook pancakes until air bubbles appear on top; flip and cook other side. Serve pancakes topped with a pat of butter and warm maple syrup. Makes about 10 pancakes.

Add your recipe card and two or three mix-and-match
ceramic bowls from your favorite thrift shop.

Harvest Soup Mix

Makes 16 one-cup servings

3/4 c. dried split peas
1/3 c. plus 2 T. beef boullion
    granules
1/2 c. pearled barley
3/4 c. dried lentils

1/2 c. dried, minced onion
3/4 c. long-grain wild rice
3/4 c. tiny bowtie or alphabet
    pasta

Blend together all ingredients and place in a one-quart wide-mouth canning jar; add lid. Tie on a gift card with instructions.

Instructions:

Place soup mix in a large stockpot. Stir in 3 quarts of water, a 28-ounce can of diced tomatoes, undrained, and 1-1/2 pounds of stew beef, browned. Bring to a boil, then reduce heat and simmer, covered, for one to 2 hours or until peas, lentils and rice are tender.

Fill a bushel basket with all the flavors of Fall...
apples, squash, tiny pumpkins and gourds, a gallon of
apple cider and Apple Dapple Muffin Mix. Tuck in
a few colorful leaves before giving.

Apple Dapple Muffin Mix

Makes one dozen

2 c. self-rising flour
1/2 c. sugar
1/4 c. brown sugar, packed

2 t. cinnamon
1/4 t. nutmeg
1 c. dried apple, chopped

Combine ingredients together; store in an airtight container. Attach instructions.

Instructions:

In a large mixing bowl, combine mix, one egg, 3/4 cup milk and 1/4 cup oil; stir until just moistened. Fill greased muffin tins 3/4 full. Bake at 400 degrees until golden, about 15 to 18 minutes. Makes 12.

Make Friendship Scone Mix everyone's favorite by adding 1/2 cup dried cranberries, white chocolate chips, chocolate chunks, walnuts or raisins...place them in a plastic bag and tie onto the jar to stir in before baking.

Friendship Scone Mix

Makes 8 scones

1-3/4 c. all-purpose flour
1 T. baking powder
1/2 t. salt
1 c. quick-cooking oats, uncooked

1/2 c. chopped walnuts
1/3 c. mini semi-sweet chocolate
chips

Combine flour, baking powder and salt together in a large mixing bowl; stir in remaining ingredients. Mix well. Store in an airtight container in a cool, dry place. Attach instructions.

Instructions:

Place scone mix in a large mixing bowl; cut in 1/2 cup butter until mixture resembles coarse crumbs. In a separate bowl, whisk together 1/4 cup milk with one egg; add to crumb mixture until just moistened. Knead gently on a lightly floured surface 8 to 10 times; pat dough into an 8-inch circle. Cut into 8 wedges; place on a lightly greased baking sheet. Bake at 375 degrees until golden, about 10 to 12 minutes. Serve warm. Makes 8.

Add smiles to this gift package by including extra
mini marshmallows so everyone can have seconds.

Marshmallow Cocoa Mix

25-oz. pkg. powdered milk
1-1/2 c. powdered non-dairy
    creamer

3 c. hot chocolate mix
1-1/2 c. powdered sugar
2 c. mini marshmallows

Combine ingredients; equally divide into 4, one-quart jars. Attach gift tags with instructions to each.

Instructions:

Combine 1/2 cup mix with one cup boiling water. Makes one serving.

Decorate a Mason jar filled with Cinna-Mocha Mix
with a pretty plaid ribbon.

Cinna-Mocha Mix

Makes 14 servings

1-3/4 c. powdered non-dairy
   creamer
3/4 c. sugar
1/2 c. baking cocoa
1/3 c. instant coffee granules

1/4 c. brown sugar, packed
1 t. cinnamon
1/4 t. salt
1/4 t. nutmeg

Place all ingredients in a blender or food processor and pulse until finely ground. Store in an airtight container; attach instructions.

Instructions:

To serve, stir 1/4 cup mix into 3/4 cup boiling water.

Place Homecoming Cobbler Mix inside a new mailbox
and deliver to friends in a brand new home...tuck in
some address stickers for the mailbox too!

Homecoming Cobbler Mix

Makes 8 to 10 servings

1 c. all-purpose flour
1 t. baking powder
1 c. sugar

1 t. vanilla powder
4 c. fresh berries

Combine flour, baking powder, sugar and vanilla powder; spoon into a plastic zipping bag. Place berries in a basket; attach instructions.

Instructions:

Combine berries, 1/4 cup orange juice, 1/4 cup sugar and one teaspoon cinnamon; spread in an ungreased 13"x9" baking pan. In a medium mixing bowl, whisk one cup melted butter and one egg together; stir in cobbler mix. Drop by tablespoonfuls onto fruit mixture; bake at 375 degrees for 35 to 45 minutes. Cool for 15 minutes before serving.

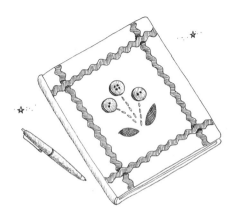

Bring a special gift to the next big celebration. Purchase
a blank journal and fill in pages with a fun theme like,
"50 Fun Memories" for a 50th anniversary party or "40 Reasons
You're the Best" for a 40th birthday. Add stickers, drawings
and photos...they'll treasure it forever!

Celebration Cherry Bread Mix

Makes 2 loaves

2-1/2 c. all-purpose flour
1 t. baking powder
1 t. baking soda
1 t. cinnamon
1/4 t. nutmeg

1/2 t. salt
1 c. quick-cooking oats, uncooked
3/4 c. dried cherries
3/4 c. sweetened, dried
   cranberries

Combine flour, baking powder, baking soda, cinnamon, nutmeg and salt together in a large mixing bowl; mix well. Add remaining ingredients; toss until blended. Place mixture in a plastic zipping bag or other airtight container; attach instructions. Store in a cool, dry place.

Instructions:

Whisk 3/4 cup honey, 3/4 cup milk, 3/4 cup melted butter and 2 beaten eggs together; set aside. Place mix in a large mixing bowl; add honey mixture, stirring until just moistened. Pour batter equally into 2 greased 8"x4" loaf pans; bake at 350 degrees for 35 to 40 minutes or until a toothpick inserted in the center removes clean. Cool on wire rack. Serves 16.

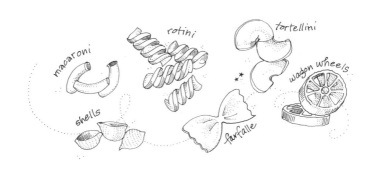

macaroni

rotini

tortellini

wagon wheels

shells

farfalle

Pick your pasta! Give Spaghetti Sauce Spice Blend with
a large glass jar filled with a variety of noodles...try layering
macaroni, rotini, tortellini, shells and wagon wheels.

Spaghetti Sauce Spice Blend

Makes 4 servings

1/4 c. celery salt
1 T. dried basil
1 T. dried oregano
1 T. dried parsley

1 T. garlic powder
1 T. onion salt
1 T. sugar
1 T. pepper

Mix ingredients together; place in an airtight container. Shake before using. Attach instructions.

Instructions:

To make spaghetti sauce, whisk an 8-ounce can tomatoes with 1/4 cup spice blend in a saucepan; simmer for 30 minutes. Pour over an 8-ounce package of pasta, cooked. Serves 4.

Make a warm scarf out of old wool sweaters in no time. Simply wash them in hot water several times and run them through a hot dryer...this turns the wool into felt. Cut out squares and sew the ends together with chunky yarn to make a patchwork scarf. Wrap around a soup mix and take to a friend on the first day of winter.

Mushroom-Barley Soup Mix

Makes 4 servings

1/2 c. pearled barley
1/4 c. dried mushroom slices
2 T. dried, minced onion
1/4 c. dried carrot slices
2 T. dried parsley

2 T. dill weed
1/2 t. garlic salt
2 bay leaves
2 t. beef bouillon granules

Combine ingredients in an airtight container; store in a cool, dark cupboard. Attach instructions.

Instructions:

Add mix to one quart boiling water or beef broth; reduce heat and simmer until barley is tender. Remove bay leaves before serving. Makes 4 servings.

Use heart, diamond, club and spade cookie cutters to cut out
Cayenne Cheddar Crackers...deliver with a package of
new playing cards to your favorite bridge partner.

Cayenne Cheddar Crackers

Makes 4 dozen

2 c. all-purpose flour
1 t. salt
1/4 t. cayenne pepper
1/4 t. dry mustard

3/4 c. chilled butter
1/2 c. shredded Cheddar cheese
6 to 8 T. cold water

Combine flour and seasonings in a mixing bowl; cut in butter with a pastry cutter until coarse crumbs form. Stir in Cheddar cheese and just enough water to hold the dough together; shape into a ball and wrap in plastic wrap. Refrigerate dough for at least 30 minutes. Roll dough out on a lightly floured surface into a 16"x12" rectangle; cut into 3"x1" strips using a sharp knife or pizza cutter. Place on parchment paper-lined baking sheets; bake at 350 degrees for 10 to 12 minutes. Cool; store in airtight containers.

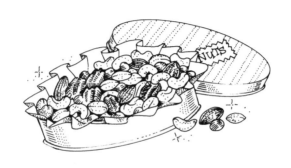

Add a snack-size gift bag of these special nuts
to a plate of Christmas cookies.

Spiced Christmas Cashews

Makes about 3-1/2 cups

1 egg white
1 T. water
2 9-3/4 oz. cans salted cashews
1/3 c. sugar

1 T. chili powder
2 t. salt
2 t. ground cumin
1/2 t. cayenne pepper

Whisk together egg white and water in a large bowl. Add cashews; toss to coat. Transfer to a colander; drain for 2 minutes. In a separate bowl, combine sugar and spices; add cashews and toss to coat. Arrange in a single layer on a greased 15"x10" jelly-roll pan. Bake, uncovered, at 250 degrees for 50 to 55 minutes, stirring once. Cool on a wire rack. Store in an airtight container.

Paper muffin cup liners come in all colors and even holiday designs...great for wrapping up individual portions of party mix!

Family Favorite Party Mix

1 c. bite-size crispy wheat cereal squares
1 c. bite-size crispy rice cereal squares
1 c. bite-size crispy corn cereal squares
1 c. peanuts
1 c. pretzel sticks
1/4 c. butter, melted
2 T. Worcestershire sauce
1 t. seasoned salt
1 t. garlic salt
1 c. candy-coated chocolates
1 c. raisins

Combine cereals, nuts and pretzels in a slow cooker. Mix together butter, sauce and salts; gently stir into cereal mixture. Cover and cook on low setting for 3 to 4 hours. Uncover and cook on low setting for an additional 30 minutes; stir occasionally. Drain on paper towel-lined baking sheets; transfer to a large bowl. Cool. Add chocolates and raisins; toss to mix. Store in an airtight container.

A crock of Cheddar spread and a log of summer sausage
turns this into a welcome holiday snack package.

Spicy Chili Crackers

Makes 15 to 18 servings

16-oz. pkg. saltine crackers
1 c. olive oil
1-oz. pkg. ranch salad dressing
    mix

2 t. chili seasoning mix
1 t. garlic powder
Optional: cayenne pepper to taste

Place crackers in a large bowl; set aside. Combine remaining ingredients in a separate bowl and stir to mix. Pour over crackers in bowl; gently stir around and let stand overnight. May also be spread on a baking sheet and baked at 250 degrees for 20 to 30 minutes. Store in an airtight container.

An air-tight plastic container with a pour-top lid would be a welcome bonus to give with this tasty granola!

Nutty Skillet Granola

Makes about 7 cups

1 c. quick-cooking oats, uncooked
1 c. old-fashioned oats, uncooked
1 c. sliced almonds
1/2 c. chopped walnuts
1/2 c. chopped pecans
1/2 c. wheat germ
1/4 c. oil
1/2 c. maple syrup
3/4 c. light brown sugar, packed
1 c. raisins

In a large bowl, mix oats, nuts and wheat germ; set aside. In a large cast-iron skillet over medium heat, combine oil, maple syrup and brown sugar. Cook, stirring constantly, until brown sugar melts and mixture just begins to bubble, about 3 minutes. Add oat mixture; stir to coat completely. Reduce heat to medium-low. Cook, stirring occasionally, until mixture begins to sizzle and toast, about 3 to 4 minutes; be careful not to burn. Remove from heat; stir in raisins. Cool for 10 minutes; transfer to an airtight container. Will keep for up to 2 weeks.

Bon Voyage! Send off vacationing friends with a road trip
gift basket. Include crossword puzzles, playing cards,
magazines, juice boxes and Munch & Crunch Snack Mix...
add a road map, just in case!

Munch & Crunch Snack Mix

Makes about 5 cups

1 c. mini pretzels
1 c. corn chips
1 c. oyster crackers
1 c. pumpkin seeds, toasted
1 c. honey-roasted peanuts
2 T. margarine, melted

2 T. brown sugar, packed
1 t. Worcestershire sauce
1 t. chili powder
1/2 t. onion salt
1/2 t. cumin
1/8 t. cayenne pepper

Toss the first 5 ingredients together in a large mixing bowl; set aside.
Whisk remaining ingredients together; pour over snack mix, stirring to
coat. Spread mix in a roasting pan; bake at 300 degrees for 25 minutes,
stirring after 12 minutes. Cool completely; store in an airtight container.

Fill decorative plastic containers or plastic mixing
bowls covered with orange cellophane with
Monster Munch and Halloween stickers.

Monster Munch

9 c. cereal or small crackers of
    your choice
4 c. popped popcorn
1-1/2 c. dry-roasted peanuts
1 c. brown sugar, packed

1/2 c. butter
1/2 c. light corn syrup
1 t. vanilla extract
1/2 t. baking soda
2 c. candy-coated chocolates

Lightly grease a large roasting pan; stir in cereal or crackers, popcorn
and peanuts. In a saucepan over medium heat, mix brown sugar, butter
and corn syrup. Bring to a boil and cook, without stirring, for 5 minutes.
Remove from heat; add vanilla and baking soda. Mix well and pour
over mixture in roasting pan; toss to coat. Bake at 250 degrees for
45 minutes, stirring every 15 minutes. Cool completely; add candy,
tossing to mix. Store in an airtight container.

Fill an athletic water bottle with Healthy Day
Snack Mix and deliver with a new workout towel
to a favorite fitness friend.

Healthy Day Snack Mix

Makes about 15 cups

1/2 c. oil
1/2 c. maple syrup
1-1/2 c. brown sugar, packed
6 c. long-cooking oats, uncooked
2 c. chopped walnuts

1 c. wheat germ
1 c. flaked coconut
1 c. raisins
1 c. sweetened, dried cranberries
   or cherries

Combine oil, maple syrup and brown sugar in a microwave-safe bowl; microwave on high for 3 minutes or until sugar dissolves, stirring often. Set aside. Mix oats, walnuts, wheat germ and coconut in a large mixing bowl; pour syrup mixture on top, stirring well. Spread evenly into 2 buttered 17"x11" rimmed baking pans; bake at 350 degrees for 20 minutes, stirring once halfway through baking. Cool mixture in pans for one hour; sprinkle with raisins and cranberries and mix well. Store in airtight containers up to 2 weeks.

Easy as A-B-C! Instead of shaping Chocolate Pretzels
into traditional pretzel shapes, form dough into letters...
spell out names, "Congrats!" or "Celebrate!"

Chocolate Pretzels

Makes about 3 dozen

3/4 c. butter, softened
3/4 c. sugar
1 egg
1 t. vanilla extract
2 c. all-purpose flour

1/3 c. baking cocoa
2 t. baking powder
1 t. salt
Garnish: assorted sprinkles

Blend butter and sugar until light and fluffy; blend in egg and vanilla.
Add flour, cocoa, baking powder and salt until just blended; divide dough
in half. Wrap one half in plastic wrap; set aside. Shape remaining dough
by tablespoonfuls into 9-inch long ropes. Twist into pretzel shapes;
lightly press into sprinkles. Arrange sprinkle-side up on lightly greased
baking sheets; repeat with remaining dough. Bake at 350 degrees for
15 minutes; remove to a wire rack to cool completely.

Pair a package of 10-Minute Rice Mix with a fun kitchen timer and a quick & easy cookbook...friends can make a new tasty meal and add a side of rice in no time!

10-Minute Rice Mix

Makes about 4 cups mix

4 c. long-cooking rice, uncooked
1-1/2 oz. pkg. onion soup mix
1/4 c. dried, minced onion

1 T. dried parsley
1/4 t. garlic salt
1/4 t. salt

Combine ingredients; store in an airtight container for up to 4 months. Attach instructions.

Instructions:

Mix one cup mix with 2 cups beef broth in a 2-quart saucepan; add one tablespoon butter. Bring to a rolling boil; reduce heat. Simmer, covered, until liquid is absorbed, about 10 to 15 minutes. Makes 4 servings.

Jazz up 1-2-3 Cheesecake by adding chocolate stars on top. Just melt one cup chocolate chips with one tablespoon shortening; pour it in a jelly-roll pan lined with foil and refrigerate just until firm. Lightly grease star-shaped cookie cutters and cut out chocolate stars. Stand them in the cake so they're upright...so easy!

1-2-3 Cheesecake

Makes 8 servings

2 8-oz. pkgs. cream cheese,
   softened
1/2 c. sugar
1 t. vanilla extract

2 eggs
1/2 c. mini semi-sweet chocolate
   chips
9-inch graham cracker pie crust

Blend cream cheese, sugar and vanilla until light and fluffy; mix in
eggs. Fold in chocolate chips; spread into pie crust. Bake at 350 degrees
for 40 minutes or until center is almost set; cool to room temperature.
Refrigerate for at least 3 hours before serving.

Slip a jar of syrup into a Christmas stocking along with
a pancake mix...a welcome surprise for neighbors.

Country Cabin Pancake Syrup   *Makes about 7 cups*

2 16-oz. pkgs. dark brown sugar   4 c. water
1 c. sugar   3/4 c. corn syrup
1/2 t. salt   1 T. maple extract

Combine all ingredients except extract in a saucepan. Bring to a boil over
medium heat; boil for about 10 minutes, stirring constantly, until sugars
are dissolved and mixture is thickened. Let cool to lukewarm; stir in
extract. Place in a covered container; keep refrigerated for up to 4 weeks.

Keep an eye open for decorative glass bottles and jars
to fill with homemade food gifts like Luscious Blueberry
Syrup. Add a little white vinegar to the rinse water after
washing...they'll be sparkling!

Luscious Blueberry Syrup

Makes about 2-1/2 cups

1/2 c. sugar
1 T. cornstarch

1/3 c. water
2 c. fresh or frozen blueberries

In a saucepan over medium heat, combine sugar and cornstarch. Stir in water gradually. Add berries; bring to a boil. Boil, stirring constantly, for one minute, or until thickened. Serve warm, or pour into a covered jar and keep in the refrigerator up to several days.

A quick springtime gift. Gather a bunch of carrots, a can of pineapple and Picnic Carrot Cake Mix...tuck inside a big picnic basket filled with Easter grass.

Picnic Carrot Cake Mix

Makes 18 servings

2 c. sugar
2 t. vanilla powder
1/2 c. chopped pecans
3 c. all-purpose flour

2 t. baking soda
1 T. cinnamon
1/4 t. nutmeg
1/8 t. ground cloves

Combine ingredients together; place in a plastic zipping bag. Attach instructions.

Instructions:

Place mix in a large mixing bowl; form a well in the center. Add 1-1/2 cups oil, 3 eggs, 3 cups grated carrots and an 8-ounce can crushed pineapple; mix well. Pour into a greased 13"x9" baking pan; bake at 350 degrees for 40 to 50 minutes or until a toothpick inserted in the center tests clean. Cool. Makes 18 servings.

Add some jingle cheer to Cheery Cherry Hot Cocoa Mix.
Slip a mix inside a red paper sack, fold the top over and
punch holes across the top in one-inch intervals. Thread a
large needle with thin ribbon and weave through the
holes to close, adding jingle bells along the way.

Cheery Cherry Hot Cocoa Mix   *Makes about one cup*

3/4 c. hot chocolate mix   4 cherry-flavored licorice twists
3/4 t. cherry drink mix

Combine first 2 ingredients in a plastic zipping bag; shake to mix. Wrap licorice twists in plastic wrap; attach to mix. Tie on instructions.

Instructions:

Add 3 tablespoons mix to 3/4 cup boiling water; stir well with one licorice twist. Makes one serving.

Add a wooden honey twirler and a package of cornbread
or biscuit mix to this gift basket.

Pear Honey

8 lbs. pears, peeled and cored	20-oz. can crushed pineapple
6 lbs. sugar	10 to 12 1/2-pint canning jars
1 T. butter	and lids, sterilized

Grate pears; place in a large heavy saucepan. Add sugar and butter; mix well. Bring to a boil; boil gently for 2 hours. Stir in pineapple; boil another 5 minutes. Spoon into hot sterilized jars, leaving 1/4-inch headspace. Wipe rims; secure with lids and rings. Process in a boiling-water bath for 10 minutes; set jars on a towel to cool. Check for seals.

Tea for two! Use a paint pen to write a whimsical quote or poem around a plain white teapot and fill it with Relaxing Tea Creamer Mix. Take it along when visiting a friend on a Saturday afternoon...she'll love it!

Relaxing Tea Creamer Mix

Makes about 2 cups

1 t. cardamom
1 t. sugar
3/4 t. cinnamon
1/2 t. ground cloves

1/2 t. nutmeg
14-oz. can sweetened
   condensed milk

Stir ingredients together; cover and refrigerate for at least 24 hours. Pour into an airtight container and attach instructions. Store in refrigerator.

Instructions:

Add 2 teaspoons creamer to a cup of brewed strong black tea; stir well. Makes one serving.

Make hand-dipped waffle cones to give with
Praline Ice Cream Syrup. Just dip the top half of
waffle cones in melted chocolate chips, then roll them
in chopped peanuts or colorful sprinkles.

Praline Ice Cream Syrup

Makes 4 jars

2 c. corn syrup
1/3 c. brown sugar, packed
1/2 c. water
1-1/4 c. chopped pecans

1/2 t. vanilla extract
4 1/2-pint canning jars and
  lids, sterilized

Combine syrup, sugar and water in a saucepan; cook over medium heat and bring to a boil. Boil for one minute; remove from heat. Stir in pecans and vanilla. Pour into hot jars, leaving 1/4 inch space at the top. Secure lids; process in a boiling-water bath for 10 minutes.

Know someone who's headed off to college? Fill a backpack
with phone cards, stamps, quarters for laundry, pencils, pens,
a family picture and an easy-to-make meal like Creamy
Cheese Soup Mix...it's the next best thing to being home!

Creamy Cheese Soup Mix

Makes 10 mixes

1-1/2 oz. pkg. 4-cheese sauce
  mix
1 T. chicken bouillon granules
1/2 t. pepper
.9-oz. pkg. vegetable soup mix

1/4 c. dried parsley
3 c. powdered non-dairy
  creamer
1/4 c. cornstarch

Mix ingredients together; place a little less than 1/2 cup mix into
10 separate small jars or plastic zipping bags. Attach instructions.

Instructions:

Empty one jar or bag of mix into a bowl or large mug; stir in one cup
boiling water. Stir until thickened, about 2 to 3 minutes. Makes
one serving.

Fresh basil makes the most delicious basil butter. Measure
1-1/2 cups packed leaves, then finely chop. Add basil to
2 cups softened butter; blend well. Basil butter is tasty
on grilled foods or steamed veggies.

Italian Basil Pesto

Makes about 2 cups

1 c. fresh basil
1 c. baby spinach
2 T. garlic, minced
1/4 c. pine nuts
1/4 c. grated Romano cheese

1/2 t. salt
1/4 t. pepper
1/2 c. olive oil
1/2 c. vegetable oil

In a food processor, combine all ingredients except oils. Pulse on and off 5 to 6 times to chop basil and spinach. With the motor running, add oils in a slow stream until creamy in texture. Cover and refrigerate.

Add a selection of premium apples to your gift basket.

Best Caramel Sauce

Makes 4 to 6 servings

14-oz. pkg. caramels, unwrapped   1/3 c. milk
1/4 c. butter, sliced   1/2 t. cinnamon

Combine all ingredients in a microwave-safe bowl. Microwave on high setting for 2 to 3 minutes, stirring after each minute, until caramels are melted. Serve warm.

INDEX

INDEX

Our Story

Back in 1984, we were next-door neighbors raising our families in the little town of Delaware, Ohio. Two moms with small children, we were looking for a way to do what we loved and stay home with the kids too. We had always shared a love of home cooking and making memories with family & friends and so, after many a conversation over the backyard fence, **Gooseberry Patch** was born.

We put together our first catalog at our kitchen tables, enlisting the help of our loved ones wherever we could. From that very first mailing, we found an immediate connection with many of our customers and it wasn't long before we began receiving letters, photos and recipes from these new friends. In 1992, we put together our very first cookbook, compiled from hundreds of these recipes and, the rest, as they say, is history.

Hard to believe it's been over 30 years since those kitchen-table days! From that original little **Gooseberry Patch** family, we've grown to include an amazing group of creative folks who love cooking, decorating and creating as much as we do. Today, we're best known for our homestyle, family-friendly cookbooks, now recognized as national bestsellers.

One thing's for sure, we couldn't have done it without our friends all across the country. Each year, we're honored to turn thousands of your recipes into our collectible cookbooks. Our hope is that each book captures the stories and heart of all of you who have shared with us. Whether you've been with us since the beginning or are just discovering us, welcome to the **Gooseberry Patch** family!

Visit our website anytime
www.gooseberrypatch.com

Jo Ann & Vickie

1·800·854·6673